Editor-in-Chief and Founder:
   Lyndon H. LaRouche, Jr.
Editorial Board: *Lyndon H. LaRouche, Jr. , Helga
   Zepp-LaRouche, Robert Ingraham, Tony
   Papert, Gerald Rose, Dennis Small, Jeffrey
   Steinberg, William Wertz*
Co-Editors: *Robert Ingraham, Tony Papert*
Managing Editor: *Nancy Spannaus*
Technology: *Marsha Freeman*
Books: *Katherine Notley*
Ebooks: *Richard Burden*
Graphics: *Alan Yue*
Photos: *Stuart Lewis*
Circulation Manager: *Stanley Ezrol*

INTELLIGENCE DIRECTORS
Counterintelligence: *Jeffrey Steinberg, Michele
   Steinberg*
Economics: *John Hoefle, Marcia Merry Baker,
   Paul Gallagher*
History: *Anton Chaitkin*
Ibero-America: *Dennis Small*
Russia and Eastern Europe: *Rachel Douglas*
United States: *Debra Freeman*

INTERNATIONAL BUREAUS
Bogotá: *Miriam Redondo*
Berlin: *Rainer Apel*
Copenhagen: *Tom Gillesberg*
Houston: *Harley Schlanger*
Lima: *Sara Madueño*
Melbourne: *Robert Barwick*
Mexico City: *Gerardo Castilleja Chávez*
New Delhi: *Ramtanu Maitra*
Paris: *Christine Bierre*
Stockholm: *Ulf Sandmark*
United Nations, N.Y.C.: *Leni Rubinstein*
Washington, D.C.: *William Jones*
Wiesbaden: *Göran Haglund*

ON THE WEB
e-mail: eirns@larouchepub.com
www.larouchepub.com
www.executiveintelligencereview.com
www.larouchepub.com/eiw
Webmaster: *John Sigerson*
Assistant Webmaster: *George Hollis*
Editor, Arabic-language edition: *Hussein Askary*

EIR (ISSN 0273-6314) *is published weekly
(50 issues), by EIR News Service, Inc.,
P.O. Box 17390, Washington, D.C. 20041-0390.
(703) 777-9451 ext. 415*

European Headquarters: E.I.R. GmbH, Postfach
Bahnstrasse 9a, D-65205, Wiesbaden, Germany
Tel: 49-611-73650
Homepage: http://www.eirna.com
e-mail: eirna@eirna.com
Director: Georg Neudecker

Montreal, Canada: 514-461-1557

Denmark: EIR - Danmark, Sankt Knuds Vej 11,
basement left, DK-1903 Frederiksberg, Denmark.
Tel.: +45 35 43 60 40, Fax: +45 35 43 87 57. e-mail:
eirdk@hotmail.com.

Mexico City: EIR, Sor Juana Inés de la Cruz 242-2
Col. Agricultura C.P. 11360
Delegación M. Hidalgo, México D.F.
Tel. (5525) 5318-2301
eirmexico@gmail.com

Canada Post Publication Sales Agreement
#40683579

Postmaster: Send all address changes to *EIR*, P.O.
Box 17390, Washington, D.C. 20041-0390.

Signed articles in *EIR* represent the views of the
authors, and not necessarily those of the Editorial
Board.

Choose Principle

Choose Principle

Lyndon LaRouche spoke to the following effect to the LaRouchePAC Policy Committee on Oct. 17.

Don't just give the name; find what the cause is, and in this case, the cause is these principles.

What you have to do, is you have to use the principle as such, and this is often not done, or it's done badly, in election campaigns. The point here is to get the election of the principle. The election of the principle, and let the principle define what the action is. Alexander Hamilton, for example: that's perfect. He's dead, right? But you can still use him as a leader, by saying, he did this, and now, I've done a supporting effort on the same issue with my "Four Laws." But the point is, you've got to get the principle in there. It's not the person; it's the principle. And the principle is carried by the person. If the thing is done competently, that is what works.

The point is, Hamilton's tradition and his policies, are policies that should be the Presidential policies of the United States.

And the point is what we're proposing on the use of my name, is a feasible idea. I'm just qualifying what makes it a feasible idea.

What you have is a policy: Alexander Hamilton's policy, as expressed now, in current times; that's what you want. Use my name, to emphasize Alexander Hamilton's name as being the figure which should be the guiding figure for the entire nation. I can make it clear; I can do it. That I know how to do. Most people don't; they get jammed up on interpretation.

He was the leading figure in American history, in the earliest part. And during the Twentieth Century, I have been a leading figure in the United States. I am now saying that the Alexander Hamilton law, as expressed in the following terms, in my Four Laws, is what has to be done for the nation.

And we've already got the policy on the books, because we've got the law that was presented in my name, more than two years ago. And that law is the law that should be the guiding law for the defining of the law of the United States as such.

Say Alexander Hamilton, and Hamilton's law and accomplishments are the things we point to,— then we use what I have done, which was done just a little over two years ago. I defined that *afresh*, which nobody else has done, except in my name. That's the way to look at it.

What I said is very simple. I, in 2014, presented a case, a policy case, for the people of the United States. That's what I did. No one else has done exactly what I did. However, I'm not assured to be running around indefinitely. The point is simply to get a policy, a policy which in this case has existed, and this is to be presented *as the policy.* It's not a matter of personality as such; it's a matter of identifying the policy. And what I did over two years ago, is exactly what the policy should be. Nothing less, nor anything more.

I was the one who defined the "Four Laws." And I'm presenting these laws as a correction, to correct and eliminate the mistakes which have been sustained or introduced. Which are mistakes. In other words, the policy is what is considered. And the policy has a supporter. And I'm the only one who did the statement on Alexander Hamilton's laws, as defined over two years ago. And this process defies all of the kinds of mishmash which have been in the electoral process recently. Period.

I have presented here, a statement. That statement has an unique characteristic of its own. It is *that* approach which could win the case. The main thing is, the United States was founded on laws which were created by Alexander Hamilton. In my recent lifetime, I have been a leading figure in exposition of this principle. You want to put it very plain. The laws that we should want to have, are those of the reform which I introduced on behalf of Alexander Hamilton. That's the way to do it. And this could be a law for all nations to pick up and use.

The idea was that Alexander Hamilton was the one who defined the principle on which the laws of the United States ought to rely. And that was provided by me, by name, in the law which I introduced to practice as such.

I have instructed the candidacies in the argument that Alexander Hamilton's program, as defined, in refreshed form,— that that is what must be introduced. It's that simple. The planet needs some direction on law. And the law must be considered as the pilot law, which is Alexander Hamilton's policy, as I advised the nation to do. And it's a solution that would work.

THE FOUR NEW LAWS TO SAVE THE U.S.A. NOW!

Not an Option: An Immediate Necessity

by Lyndon H. LaRouche, Jr.

We reprint this article as it first appeared in Executive Intelligence Review in the June 13, 2014 issue.

June 10, 2014

The following statement is for immediate action by all associates in all regions of the National Caucus of Labor Committees and its associated practice. The priority is assigned to all means and measures of public action, nationally and internationally, without reservation. That priority is existential for the policies of our republic, and for the general information of, and by all relevant circles world-wide, beginning this date of June 8, 2014.

1. The Fact of the Matter

The economy of the United States of America, and also that of the trans-Atlantic political-economic regions of the planet: are, now, under the immediate, mortal danger of a general, physical-economic, chain-reaction breakdown-crisis of that region of this planet as a whole. The name for that direct breakdown-crisis throughout those indicated regions of the planet, is the presently ongoing introduction of a general "Bail-in" action under the several, or more governments of that region: the effect on those regions, will be comparable to the physical-economic collapse of the post-"World War I" general collapse of the economy of the German Weimar Republic: but, this time, hitting, first, the entirety of the nation-state economies of the trans-Atlantic region, rather than some defeated economies within Europe. A chain-reaction collapse, to this effect, is already accelerating with an effect on the money-systems of the nations of that region. The present acceleration of a "Bail-in" policy throughout the trans-Atlantic region, as underway now, means mass-death suddenly hitting the populations of all nations within that trans-Atlantic region: whether directly, or by "overflow."

The effects of this already prepared action by the monetarist interests of that so-designated region, will, unless stopped virtually now, will produce, in effect, an accelerating rate of genocide throughout that indicated portion of the planet immediately, but, also, with catastrophic "side effects" of comparable significance in the Eurasian regions.

The Available Remedies

The only location for the immediately necessary action which could prevent such an immediate genocide throughout the trans-Atlantic sector of the planet, requires the U.S. Government's now immediate decision *to institute four specific, cardinal measures: measures which must be fully consistent with the specific intent of the original U.S. Federal Constitution*, as had been specified by U.S. Treasury Secretary Alexander Hamilton while he remained in office: *(1) immediate re-enactment of the Glass-Steagall law instituted by U.S. President Franklin D. Roosevelt, without modification, as to principle of action. (2) A return to a system of top-down, and thoroughly defined as National Banking.*

The actually tested, successful model to be authorized is that which had been instituted, under the direction of the policies of national banking which had been actually, successfully installed under President Abraham Lincoln's superseding authority of a currency created by the Presidency of the United States (e.g. "Greenbacks"), as conducted as *a national banking-and-credit-system placed under the supervision of the Office of the Treasury Secretary of the United States.*

For the present circumstances, all other banking and currency policies, are to be superseded, or, simply, discontinued: as follows. Banks qualifying for operations under this provision, shall be assessed for their proven competence to operate as under the national authority for creating and composing the elements of this essential practice, which had been assigned, as by tradition, to the original office of Secretary of the U.S. Treasury under Alexander Hamilton. This means that the individual states of the United States are under national standards of practice, and, not any among the separate states of our nation.

(3) The purpose of the use of a Federal Credit-system, is to generate high-productivity trends in improvements of employment, with the accompanying intention, to increase the physical-economic productivity, and the standard of living of the persons and households of the United States. The creation of credit for the now urgently needed increase of the relative quality and quantity of productive employment, must be assured, this time, once more, as was done successfully under President Franklin D. Roosevelt, or by like standards of Federal practice used to create a general economic recovery of the nation, per capita, and for rate of net effects in productivity, and by reliance on the essential human principle, which distinguishes the human personality from the systemic characteristics of the lower forms of life: the net rate of increase of the energy-flux density of effective practice. This means intrinsically, a thoroughly scientific, rather than a merely mathematical one, and by the related increase of the effective energy-flux density per capita, *and for the human population when considered as each and all as a whole. The ceaseless increase of the physical-productivity of employment, accompanied by its benefits for the general welfare, are a principle of Federal law which must be a paramount standard of achievement of the nation and the individual.*[1]

(4) "Adopt a Fusion-Driver 'Crash Program.'" The essential distinction of man from all lower forms of life, hence, in practice, is that it presents the means for the perfection of the specifically affirmative aims and needs of human individual and social life. Therefore: the subject of man in the process of creation, as an affirmative identification of an affirmative statement of an absolute state of nature, is a permitted form of expression. Principles of nature are either only affirmation, or they could not be affirmatively stated among civilized human minds.

Given the circumstances of the United States, in

---

1. The substitution of "3. Cancel Green Policies ..." for the correct, "A Federal Credit-System," is a travesty against the principles of any actually scientific principle. Only affirmative identifications of "Science," could ever be allowed. Only, the previous title: "The Use of a Federal Credit System" is permitted. Eliminate all use of reference to "Green Policies": the very use of that latter reference, is a fraudulent representation.

particular, since the assassinations of President John F. Kennedy, and his brother, Robert, the rapid increase required for even any recovery of the U.S. economy, since that time, requires nothing less than measures taken and executed by President Franklin D. Roosevelt during his actual term in office. The victims of the evil brought upon the United States and its population since the strange death of President Harding, under Presidents Calvin Coolidge and Herbert Hoover (like the terrible effects of the Bush-Cheney and Barack Obama administrations, presently) require remedies comparable to those of President Franklin Roosevelt while he were in office.

This means emergency relief measures, including sensible temporary recovery measures, required to stem the tide of death left by the Coolidge-Hoover regimes: measures required to preserve the dignity of what were otherwise the unemployed, while building up the most powerful economic and warfare capabilities assembled under the President Franklin Roosevelt Presidency for as long as he remained alive in office. This meant the mustering of the power of nuclear power, then, and means thermonuclear fusion now. Without that intent and its accomplishment, the population of the United States in particular, faces, now, immediately, the most monstrous disaster in its history to date. In principle, without a Presidency suited to remove and dump the worst effects felt presently, those created presently by the Bush-Cheney and Obama Presidencies, the United States were soon finished, beginning with the mass-death of the U.S. population under the Obama Administration's recent and now accelerated policies of practice.

There are certain policies which are most notably required, on that account, now, as follows:

Vernadsky on Man & Creation

V.I. Vernadsky's systemic principle of human nature, is a universal principle, which is uniquely specific to the crucial factor of the existence of the human species. For example: "time" and "space" do not actually exist as a set of metrical principles of the Solar system; their only admissible employment is for purposes of communication is essentially nominal presumption. Since competent science for today can be expressed only in terms of the unique characteristic of the human species' role within the known aspects of the universe, the human principle is the only true principle known to us for practice: the notions of space and time are merely useful imageries:

Rather:

The essential characteristic of the human species, is its distinction from all other species of living processes: that, as a matter of principle, which is, rooted scientifically, for all competent modern science, on the foundations of the principles set forth by Filippo Brunelleschi (the discoverer of the ontological minimum), Nicholas of Cusa (the discovery of the ontological maximum), and the positive discovery by mankind, by Johannes Kepler, of a principle coincident with the perfected Classical human singing scale adopted by Kepler, and the elementary measure of the Solar System within the still larger universe of the Galaxy, and higher orders in the universe.

Or, similarly, later, the modern physical-scientific standard implicit in the argument of Bernhard Riemann, the actual minimum (echoing the principle of Brunelleschi), of Max Planck, the actual maximum of the present maximum, that of Albert Einstein; and, the relatively latest, consequent implications of the definition of human life by Vladimir Ivanovich Vernadsky. These values are, each relative absolutes of measurement of man's role within the knowledge of the universe.

This set of facts pertains to the inherent fraud of the merely mathematicians and the modernist "musical performers" since the standard of the relevant paragon for music, Johannes Brahms (prior to the degenerates, such as the merely mathematicians, such as David Hilbert and the true model for every modern Satan, such as Bertrand Russell, or Tony Blair).

The knowable measure, in principle, of the difference between man and all among the lower forms of life, is found in what has been usefully regarded as the naturally upward evolution of the human species, in contrast to all other known categories of living species. The standard of measurement of these compared relationships, is that mankind is enabled to evolve upward, and that categorically, by those voluntarily noëtic powers of the human individual will.

Except when mankind appears in a morally and physically degenerate state of behavior, such as within the cultures of the tyrants Zeus, the Roman Empire, and the British empire, presently: all actually sane cultures of mankind, have appeared, this far, in a certain fact of evolutionary progress from the quality of an inferior, to a superior species. This, when considered in terms of efficient effects, corresponds, within the domain of a living human practice of chemistry, to a form of systemic advances, even now leaps, in the chemical energy-flux density of society's increase of the effective energy-flux-density of scientific and comparable expressions of leaps in progress of the species itself: in short, a universal physical principle of human progress.

The healthy human culture, such as that of Christianity, if they warrant this affirmation of such a devotion, for example, represents a society which is increasing the powers of its productive abilities for progress, to an ever higher level of per-capita existence. The contrary cases, "the so-called zero-growth" scourges, such as the current British empire are, systemically, a true model consistent with the tyrannies of a Zeus, or, a Roman Empire, or a British (better said) "brutish" empire, such as the types, for us in the United States, of the Bush-Cheney and Obama administrations, whose characteristic has been, concordant with that of such frankly Satanic models as that of Rome and the British empire presently, a shrinking human population of the planet, a population being degraded presently in respect to its intellectual and physical productivity, as under those U.S. Presidencies, most recently.

Chemistry: The Yardstick of History

We call it "chemistry." Mankind's progress, as measured rather simply as a species, is expressed typically in the rising power of the principle of human life, over the abilities of animal life generally, and relatively absolute superiority over the powers of non-living processes to achieve within mankind's willful intervention to that intended effect. *Progress exists so only under a continuing, progressive increase of the productive and related powers of the human species. That progress defines the absolute distinction of the human species from all others presently known to us. A government of people based on a policy of "zero-population growth and per capita standard of human life" is a moral, and practical abomination.*

Man is mankind's only true measure of the history of our Solar system, and what reposes within it. That is the same thing, as the most honored meaning and endless achievement of the human species, now within nearby Solar space, heading upward to mastery over the Sun and its Solar system, the one discovered (uniquely, as a matter of fact), by Johannes Kepler.

A Fusion economy, is the presently urgent next step, and standard, for man's gains of power within the Solar system, and, later, beyond.

EIRContents

www.larouchepub.com Volume 43, Number 43, October 21, 2016

Cover This Week

Lyndon H. LaRouche, Jr.

EIRNS/Stuart Lewis

A New Financial Architecture and A Classical-Cultural Renaissance Are Urgently Needed

by Helga Zepp-LaRouche

Helga Zepp-LaRouche delivered the following keynote address, "A New Financial Architecture and a Classical-Cultural Renaissance Are Urgently Needed," to an October 13 video-conference on "The BRICS Summit: Alternatives for a World in Crisis," held with simultaneous meetings in Guatemala City, Mexico City, and Lima, Peru. The gatherings in those three cities were linked live by Google Hangouts on Air, and a panel discussion followed Mrs. Zepp-LaRouche's remarks, with Dr. Mario Roberto Morales (Professor at San Carlos University, Guatemala), Dr. Horacio Sanchez Barcenas (Vice President of the National Federation of Economists, Mexico), and Luis Vasquez Medina (EIR, Peru). The event was sponsored by the Center for Latin American Studies of the Department of Political Science of San Carlos University, the Schiller Institute, and Executive Intelligence Review. *Mrs. Zepp-LaRouche had pretaped her address on Oct. 6.*

Good day. Thank you so much for inviting me to address your conference. The world is in a very, very dangerous situation. Everybody who watches the strategic developments every day can see how the confrontation between the United States and Russia is increasing. Just a few days ago, the official coordinator for the cooperation with Russia of the German government said on the

EIRNS/Stuart Lewis
Helga Zepp-LaRouche

Second Channel of German TV, that a direct military confrontation between the United States and Russia can no longer be excluded. Now, it's not that this is something new, but the fact that a representative of the German government said it, is new. What he referred to was the complete breakdown of negotiations between Russia and the United States over the Syria crisis. And there is the immediate danger of an escalation if the policies of such people as General Petraeus or Sen. John McCain were implemented.

And I think everybody knows that if it came to war between Russia and the United States, it would be a global war, and it would lead to the annihilation of all of mankind, in all likelihood.

Now, there is a second danger to civilization which could also lead in the end to a nuclear war, and that is that we are about to face a total collapse of the trans-Atlantic financial system, much, much worse than 2008. The IMF has named Deutsche Bank as *the* bank with the most risk in the whole global financial system, and it depends on what will be the outcome of both the IMF/World Bank annual meeting in Washington right now, where the CEO of Deutsche Bank, John Cryan, went; but, also at the same time, to negotiate with the Department of Justice to reduce the fine of $14 billion which the DOJ had fined Deutsche Bank for criminal manipulations before the secondary mortgage crisis in

2007-2008, from $14 billion to only $5 billion, because $14 billion would mean de facto the insolvency of Deutsche Bank.

Now, the German daily *Die Welt* said what Cryan is doing is a "chicken game"; that Deutsche Bank has $42 trillion worth in outstanding derivatives, and that is enough, if Deutsche Bank goes bankrupt, to bring down the entire financial system. And according to the old wisdom, if you have enough debt, you can impose the conditions of how this debt will be renegotiated; but *Die Welt* basically said, this is a chicken game which nobody would survive.

Alexander Hamilton's First Bank of the United States (1797-1811).
CC/Davidt8

Now, Deutsche Bank is maybe the worst case, but by far not the only one. Deutsche Bank, as I said, has $42 trillion in outstanding derivatives: that is about 12 times the entire GDP of the German economy per year, and it's still about 3 to 4 times the GDP of the entire European Union. Therefore, it is obvious that if Deutsche Bank collapses, neither the bail-in law—which is by now law in the entire European Union—nor the bail-out would be sufficient to solve the problem. And if you look at the engagement of these derivatives with the banks which are counterparty to Deutsche Bank, it involves the entire too-big-to-fail banking system of the trans-Atlantic system; and if Deutsche Bank goes without state intervention (and that is obviously not the solution either) it could be like a super-nova, basically evaporating in a very brief time.

There Is a Remedy

A similar situation is true for the Italian banks, and for the British banks after the Brexit—and one should not overlook that all of these banks have large fines to pay for crimes. Deutsche Bank had to pay because they manipulated and cheated the customers in the real-estate market in the United States. Wells Fargo just had a hearing in the U.S. Congress because they set up 2 million fraudulent, fictitious bank accounts to steal. Then you have HongShang Banking Corporation, which is openly laundering the entire drug money of the Mexican drug mafia. They all were involved in the LIBOR manipulation, which caused the three-digit billion losses for the customers.

We are for sure heading towards an October crisis. This is not going to be a crisis after the U.S. election: This is now. And all the means of the central banks: quantitative easing they have been doing since 2008; negative interest rates, which kills the savings of the population; and now they're talking about "helicopter money," which is really the last straw. All of these tools do not function any more.

There is a remedy, and that is, you have to implement immediately the Glass-Steagall banking separation law, exactly what Franklin D. Roosevelt did in 1933. Lyndon LaRouche has enlarged that conception to say, we need Glass-Steagall, that is, you have to write off the speculative part of the banks; but then you have a lack of liquidity and therefore, you have to have a credit system in the tradition of Alexander Hamilton, which issues new, large credits for productive investments. But you also have to increase the productivity of the economy, and you have to have a science driver; and the best way for that is international space cooperation and vanguard technologies which go along with that.

We also need what Roosevelt did at the time: a Pecora Commission. Pecora was the New York State Attorney, who investigated the CEOs of the Wall Street banks under oath at the time, to then send many of them to jail. And as a leading banker contact told us, if you don't do that, you cannot reinstate the confidence in the banks, because people have completely lost confidence in the system, which is obviously more criminal than not.

There is good reason that this can be done. Because in the United States, both parties, the Republicans and the Democrats, have the Glass-Steagall Act in their platforms; and despite the fact that Hillary Clinton is not for Glass-Steagall, it is important that in times of crisis, such provisions are there. And there is a renewed optimism that you can mobilize the Congress, even if normally people have little hope that the Congress will do something useful. They just did by voting up the JASTA bill overriding the veto of President Obama in respect of the ability of the families of the victims of September 11th, to sue the Saudi government. This is a tremendous victory, because what was victorious in this situation was a sense for justice: That it was completely unjust that the victims of the September 11th terrorist attack would not have the ability, and the families in particular would not have the ability, to bring the criminals responsible for that terrorist act to court. And that has now occurred, and there is a tremendous sense that you can move, once people are united for a good plan, and once they act together.

Now, there is an equal yearning for justice concerning the banking system. The banking system which has provided unbelievable profits for a few; where bankers who provably are criminal can get away with bonuses of hundreds of millions of dollars, while the people they are looting, more and more of them become completely impoverished.

The other important aspect about this is that the alternative financial system is already in place. Since 2013, when President Xi Jinping announced the New Silk Road, there has been an unbelievable development, in the tradition of the ancient Silk Road of 2,000 years ago during the Han Dynasty, which at that time was an immense exchange, not only of goods, but of culture, of ideas, and most importantly of technologies, of the ability to produce silk, to make porcelain, and other such vanguard technologies of that time; the idea

Xinhua/Zhu Xiang

First direct cargo train leaving Zhengzhou for Europe, July 18, 2013. Zhengzhou is the capital of China's Henan Province.

is now that the same kind of exchange has been occurring for three years among the nations of the New Silk Road, but with modern technologies.

This is the largest infrastructure plan in all of human history: It's about twelve times larger than the Marshall Plan which helped to reconstruct Europe after the Second World War, in terms of actual buying power. It right now encompasses $1.4 trillion; it already involves 43% of the world economy, and 4.4 *billion* people. Seventy countries are cooperating around it. It is the only long-term development strategy in the world right now, under the leadership of China. As a matter of fact, it's the only strategic plan to overcome this present geopolitical confrontation I mentioned in the beginning, because it is based on the idea of a "win-win cooperation" of all countries on this planet.

What Really is the New Silk Road?

Very important, in respect to the financial crisis, these countries have started to set up an alternative financial system. They have started the Asian Infrastructure Investment Bank (AIIB), where immediately about 70 countries wanted to be founding members, despite enormous pressure from the United States not to do so. Even close allies of the United States, like Great Britain, Japan, South Korea, Germany, France, and Canada, all wanted to be founding members of this new bank, which has a starting capital of $100 billion, which can be expanded, and will be. They also have created the New Development Bank, that is the bank of the BRICS countries; the New Silk Road Fund of $40 billion; the Maritime Silk Road Fund; the Shanghai Cooperation Organization has created a new bank; and they have created something called the Contingency Reserve Arrangement which began as a pool of $100 billion, helping the BRICS countries and other developing countries to fend off manipulative speculative attacks like those of George Soros and other speculators.

It is very important that this idea of the New Silk Road is expanding with an unbelievable speed, and many countries, not only in Asia, but also in, for example, Eastern and Central Europe, are picking up on it. There is now a cooperation between China and Greece, Serbia, Hungary, the Czech Republic and even Poland, all working on high-speed trains and infrastructure cooperation. And the idea is to extend this kind of a New Silk Road into the Middle East and into Africa; to address the very, very dramatic situation there, to reconstruct the Middle East after the war, and to develop Africa, and also to end the refugee crisis, which is one of the largest humanitarian crises in the world ever; to create conditions where Africa and Southwest Asia are being industrialized so that people do not want to leave their homes, but rather, to help to build up their nations.

All of this is not just business. The Silk Road is by no means only infrastructure in the narrow sense, connecting A to B through trains and ships, but it is also not just a replacement of American imperialism by Chinese imperialism, which is what some media are trying to insinuate. The New Silk Road, put on the agenda by China, is truly a completely different model of cooperation among states. It is based on dialogue, partnership, and cooperation; and China does not want to be a new hegemon, but wants to have cooperation with all coun-

Imaginary portrait of Confucius, illustrating the frontispiece of the book Confucius Sinarum Philosophus, *Paris, 1687. The linear perspective is a feature of European art.*

tries based on a "win-win" mutual benefit, where each country has its own advantage.

China has said many times—as a matter of fact, Xi Jinping has used the formulation that what is needed is a "community of shared destiny." Now, this is what the Schiller Institute has promoted for 25 years, when we proposed the Eurasian Land-Bridge when the Soviet Union collapsed, and expanded it in the 25 years since, that the Silk Road must become the World Land-Bridge. We always have said that we need a completely new paradigm based on "win-win cooperation"; and that is exactly what is now being pushed by China.

Now people always have suspicions: "what is the real aim of China?" But I have come to the absolute conclusion, that China *means* exactly what they're saying; that the world must not be run on the basis of a zero-sum game, but on the idea of a harmony of all nations.

Now, 2016 is the 2,567th birthday of Confucius, and you have right now a total revival of Confucian philosophy, in all of China, in all schools, universities, cities; and there is right now a two-and-a-half-thousand-year-old history of Confucian tradition in China, with the very short exception of the ten years of the Cultural Revolution. And that has shaped the Chinese mind to a very large extent—the Confucian idea that the world should be organized in a harmonious way, by allowing the harmonious development of all nations, of all families, of all individuals; and that a country cannot do well, if its neighbors are not doing well. The idea of Confucius, that politics must be based on love, now that is associated with the idea that politics has only one aim, and that is the happiness of people, an idea which used to belong the American Declaration of Independence, and an idea which is also very well known in the history of European humanism.

Confucius also taught that people have to have a lifelong learning, and that they should perfect themselves without limit, and that the highest ideal of man is the *chun tzu*, the wise man who perfects himself in the highest degree. And out of this comes the idea that the sage king is morally much more attractive than the hegemon. This is the same idea as Plato's "philosopher king," that only the wisest and most moral people should rule.

Classical Culture

Now, while the hegemon rules by forcing the underlings into submission, the wise king and the wise leadership elevate the people through inspiration. At the recent G20 meeting in Hangzhou, which occurred for the first time under the leadership of China, they have made a wonderful proposal to place the whole world economy on the basis of innovation, and to share whatever scientific and technological breakthroughs are made, immediately, with all other nations, but especially the developing nations, so that their development is not held up.

Since then, they have announced scientific and technological cooperation among the countries along the New Silk Road; they have opened up science and technology parks, and huge exchanges of scientists and youth, in order to spread these ideas in the quickest possible way. All of these policies are a reflection of the Confucian philosophy.

If you study it more closely, you will realize there is a tremendous affinity between Confucian thinking and European humanism. They are much closer and much more related than most people are aware. While in China, a Confucian Renaissance is fully underway, it is the West which is in urgent need of such a cultural renaissance.

The Western world has plunged into a terrible moral degeneracy and decadence: If you look at the drug addiction, for example—well, the case of Mexico, for example, is famous: The drug lords have taken over much of the country. But in the United States, drug addiction is the most important cause for the rising suicide rate which has quadrupled since 2001, since Bush came into office; suicides in all age groups. If you look at the violence in the United States, but also in other Western parts, you have the police violence, you have the school shootings, you have pornography, and you have the total brutalization of behavior, which almost is a breakdown of civilized relations among people. I don't want to go into this more deeply, because you all know it.

Scholars at an Abbasid library. Illustration for the Maqamat *of al-Hariri by Yahya Ibn Mahmud al-Wasiti, Baghdad, 1237 AD.*

So we need urgently, if you want to save humanity, we need a Renaissance of Classical culture. We have to go back to an image of Man which emphasizes that which separates Man from all other living species, and that is the creativity of the mind of the human being. The problem with popular culture is that it *de*-emphasizes this creativity. Pop music, for example, if young people go to discos, it almost always goes along with drug consumption, with something which destroys the creative faculties of the mind.

We need a Classical culture which emphasizes the beauty of the best traditions of Greece: for example, Greek architecture, Greek historical dramas, Greek philosophy; but also the beauty of Dante, of Petrarca, of the Italian Renaissance; in the Spanish culture, of the Andalusian renaissance, of Cervantes, of Goya; in Germany, Schiller, Beethoven, and many other great thinkers.

Now, why is Classical culture so absolutely important? Rather than being a soap opera, where you add irrational emotions one after the other, without rhythm or rhyme, you have in Classical culture either a poetical or a musical idea, and then, according to very strict principles of composition, you develop that idea until it is exhausted, in a thorough-compositional way; and then you come to a conclusion on a higher level of reason. And when you train your mind in this way, in Classical thinking, you become more creative. And it also leads to an education of the emotions. Because if you only rely on your senses, you are just reacting. That is why Friedrich Schiller demanded the aesthetical education of Man: namely, through Classical art, the aesthetical education teaches Man to feel more noble and to educate your emotions up to the level of reason, so that you can blindly follow your impulses because they will never tell you anything different than what reason commands. This is why we have to reintroduce beauty into art, and the great German poet Friedrich Schiller said "Art which is not beautiful should not be called art."

In the Greek Classical period, you had the ideal of the identity of the beautiful, the truthful, and the good. And you cannot be truthful if you are not trying to develop the idea of beauty, and you cannot develop the good without being truthful. So there is an inner connection between these, because they address the same faculty in the human mind.

Man's Destiny

The future of mankind very clearly will be in space. If you look at the evolution of man, or even of life as it developed through photosynthesis from the oceans to land, from lower to higher species, and eventually the creative mankind: Man settled at the rivers and oceans first; then through infrastructure development, opened up the landlocked areas of continents. And now, with the New Silk Road, we are completing that phase of the evolution, where Man through infrastructure, develops the landlocked areas of all continents. And the natural extension of that infrastructure development will be the opening-up of near space, probably first a colony on the Moon, and that will be the launching pad for future space operations as our energy sources become more dense, and we will even be able to understand much better what is the position of our planet in the Solar System, and in the Galaxy; and we will develop a much deeper understanding of the laws of the universe and the relationship of creative mentation to that Universe, because our mind is obviously not outside of the Universe, but it's part of the Universe, and it is the most developed part.

A lot more studies have to made about that connection between the mind and the universe at large, and the better we understand that connection, the more rational we will become as a human species. The great German space scientist Krafft Ehricke developed the beautiful notion of the "extraterrestrial imperative," saying that Man only becomes truly adult when we try to understand and conquer space more deeply, because Man will only become fully rational when we do that. And Krafft Ehricke, who was a close friend of ours, said at the end of his life, that the importance of great Classical art was absolutely crucial, because if science is developed, that does not yet say whether it's applied for something good, or for something bad; it is always Man who applies that science which makes the difference. And therefore, the aesthetical and moral education to beauty and to the good, is what will make the longevity of the human species possible.

Now, this is why we are saying, so emphatically, that the economic development of the New Silk Road must be combined with a Classical Renaissance of Classical culture, and that we must bring forward the best traditions of each culture, of Chinese poetry and philosophy, of Chinese painting, of Indian philosophy, of wonderful African philosophical contributions from the time of Timbuktu; of other great cultures, which each, at one point had a high phase in their culture, like the Arab Renaissance of the Abbasid Dynasty, at which point the Arab culture was the most developed.

What we have to do, is we have to make the best phases of these periods known, and then have a dialogue between these cultures, and then out of that we will generate love for the other culture; and we will indeed reach a new paradigm of civilization.

If we make that cultural universal heritage known to all children, in universal education, I think the future will be that such geniuses as Bach, Schiller, Einstein, will not be such an exception. There will never be a second Einstein, but we will have many, many geniuses because we will provide children with a much, much better opportunity to unfold all the potentials which are embedded in them.

Now, I think we are not only on the verge of a potential global war, but with the New Silk Road we are also at the edge of entering a completely new paradigm of civilization, what I like to call the "adulthood of mankind," and not behaving any longer like stupid little two-year-old boys kicking each other in the knee.

So we are really at an important historical moment, and I would ask all of you to join in a Renaissance movement, because I'm absolutely optimistic that if all good people on the planet work together to this aim, we can do it.

The Fact Is, Barack Obama Must Be Impeached!

by Dennis Speed, Oct. 18, 2016

"Now what I want is Facts. Teach these boys and girls nothing but Facts. Facts alone are wanted in life. Plant nothing else, and root out everything else. You can only form the minds of reasoning animals upon Facts: nothing else will ever be of any service to them. This is the principle on which I bring up my own children, and this is the principle on which I bring up these children. Stick to Facts, Sir!"

—Charles Dickens,
Hard Times

"The central formal problem of contemporary knowledge is that the *fact*, which naive opinion takes for the elementary or simple basis of human knowledge, proves upon critical examination to be a highly suspect authority. The concept of a 'fact', we discover through reflection, is the result of a process of judgement and therefore by no means as simple or self-evident as naive opinion assumes. In the process of judgement the experiential continuum is apparently arbitrarily bounded to form a notion of particularity from what is actually a continuous process; upon that constructed, artificed particularity of objective reference a mental construct as such is imposed. It is that mental construct which represents the best of ordinary opinion's 'hard facts'."

—Lyndon LaRouche,
"The Production of Consciousness"

Barack Obama, Thermonuclear Nero

Until September 28, it was a universally accepted "fact" that it was impossible to deploy the United States

Lyndon LaRouche

LPACTV

Congress to successfully act against Barack Obama in the interest of the American people and Republic. When the dust cleared after the vote to override Obama's veto of the Justice Against the Sponsors of Terrorism Act (JASTA), however, the Congress, particularly the entire United States Senate minus one, had joined hands in its greatest show of unity in this century to humiliate Obama—the *real* Barack Obama. They had been inspired by the families of 9/11 victims, by former senators, by their oath of office, and by an unseen, unacknowledged cultural shift in the United States, centered in Manhattan, to do what most of the Congress had secretly wished to do all along. Now, with the world placed the edge of a recklessly provoked "global thermonuclear showdown," Obama should be "overridden" out of the Presidency, deploying the power of the United States Constitution to use his latest provocation against Russia's Vladimir Putin, as the occasion to suggest that fully justified recourse.

That such an action does not appear likely or probable, though it may be absolutely necessary for the continued foreseeable survival of the planet in the short term, means that the accepted world of facts must yield to a higher platform of judgement and action. The electoral process be damned, since it has already been, once the two nominees of the Republican and Democratic parties were "chosen."

When a Russian head of state, through various diplomatic channels, makes it clear that his government views threats, such as that made by vice-President Joe Biden on Sunday's October 16th edition of *Meet The Press,* toward Russia, to be unlike those of any period other than that of the October, 1962 Cuban Missile Crisis, the first thing to realize is that the post-November 1989 period of history has been officially declared to be over. The "post-Soviet unipolar world" fantasized by the neo-conservatives of "Project for a New American Century" fame has withered away. A new period of history, either far more dangerous, or more hopeful, has begun. That apparently sudden and fundamental world-shift will not tolerate an Obama (or Clinton or Trump) at the helm of the world's most powerful but rapidly declining "superpower."

"But isn't it a fact that one of these people is going to be President of the United States for, or in the foreseeable future?" Actually, it is possible that Alexander Hamilton, the designer of the American Federal system and its first Treasury Secretary, could at last become President of the United States. Hamilton's policies, as captured in Lyndon LaRouche's Four Laws, could become, almost overnight, the dominant discussion among crucially influential portions of the citizens and

Alexander Hamilton

the electorate of the United States. The means to make such a process occur exist.

Why should LaRouche and Hamilton be read, in depth, and their ideas be mastered, as if "overnight"? The impending, momentary descent into the maelstrom of a terminal planet-wide monetary collapse of the trans-Atlantic financial system could itself, also, be the catalyst for an Obama-provoked thermonuclear war confrontation—especially because Russia, China and other states have taken steps to avert that very economic fate, and Obama's controllers are not amused. Their "old, mad, blind, despised and dying" world view asserts that if this is indeed "Götterdammerung" —the twilight of the monetary gods — then there should rather be a planet-wide thermonuclear extinction war, than that their system should be collapsed and a just community of sovereign but cooperating and prosperous nation states supersede it. Is Barack "Nero" Obama the thermonuclear pyromaniac selected for the job?

"But who would be insane enough to blow up the whole world, since that would destroy them as well?" Ask yourself: would the persons that drove the planes into the World Trade Center not have preferred to have hijacked American military planes equipped with nuclear weapons? Would they have been stopped by the consideration that using such thermonuclear weapons in a terrorist attack might start thermonuclear World War Three? Clearly, there are forces and individuals that are criminally insane enough to do so. Could that happen, has that happened, in the case of the U.S. Presidency? Was for example, the Kennedy Presidency pressured to that same effect, that is, to use nuclear weapons against the Soviet Union in October of 1962?

Fortunately for the world, Vladimir Putin is a brilliant leader of Russia. Fortunately, also, China has for over two decades, in various ways, perfected a design presented to China and the world by Lyndon LaRouche—the New Silk Road/World Land-Bridge—for the creation of a new, unique world physical-economic platform. This is to be accomplished by way of development corridors through the interiors of continents—a completely revolutionary approach to economic growth, including the technological development of Earth's atmosphere, near-Earth space, and the exploration and mining of the Moon as the extended

EIRNS

April 1994, Pobisk G. Kuznetsov, center, with Lyndon LaRouche, right, in Russia.

neighborhood of that new industrial platform. LaRouche's collaborators in Russia, particularly from the 1990s when LaRouche was made an honorary member of the Russian Academy of Sciences even as he sat in a Minnesota prison—a position not unfamiliar to the best of Russian intellectuals in their own time—had early recognized his unique contribution to physical economy and science more generally. That "fact" was registered throughout the entirety of post-1989 Russia, on top of the fact of LaRouche being the chief interlocutor for and designer of the 1983 beam-weapons policy that was termed the Strategic Defense Initiative (SDI) by the Reagan Administration. LaRouche, upon his release from his unlawful imprisonment in 1994, renewed his work in Russia. Professors Taras Muranivsky, Pobisk Kuznetsov, and Stanislav Menshikov, among others, were his collaborators. Today's Strategic Defense of the Earth (SDE) initiative on the part of Russia is a descendant of the earlier 1990s and 1980s work.

These facts are not actually unknown in the United States: they are simply denied. But the facts are not denied in Russia, and Vladimir Putin, among others, is well aware of LaRouche's true capabilities in the field of physical economy. Therefore, when LaRouche announces that he has formulated the core of Hamilton's four Reports, written by Hamilton in 1790-91 as Secretary of the Treasury of the United States to then-President Washington—dealing with manufactures, public

credit, the national bank and mint, and his opinion on the constitutionality of the national bank—into what LaRouche terms "the Four Laws," China and Russia listen. Something that, despite or perhaps because of the size of his ears, Barack Obama would find impossible to do.

The American people must have the courage to listen to LaRouche's Four Laws, to supplant the President, supersede the pornographic Presidential mule-race, and open up and read Hamilton's Reports immediately—partially, even, as a thermonuclear war-avoidance measure. Sometimes the high-profile evidence of a public commitment to vigorously change course on the part of a powerful nation's citizens, is the most effective sign one can use to change a potentially deadly adversary into a close friend. Thousands of Americans, rather than worrying about voting, should elect themselves to become true citizens of the United States by reading Hamilton's founding documents.

The solution to our present crisis, is, in fact, that search by the American people itself, for signs of intelligent life in the United States, including in the Congress. That must start with insisting that Hamilton's measures be implemented by the government on an emergency basis, which means that Congress must return at once to Washington and start by overriding Obama's certain veto of the reinstatement of the Glass-

Steagall Act, and the other measures that would be immediately required. (The fact that both the Republican and Democratic Party platforms support Glass-Steagall's reinstatement provides the stage to re-enact the JASTA legislative victory, over Obama's certain, "Governor Andros"-like imperial veto.)

The hard fact is that unless the U.S. population at large is quickly perceived to be truly deeply involved in a crash self-education course in the American Constitutional System, there is a high probability, at least according to members of the Russian government, that the October Surprise that might happen in 2016 is that neither Trump, nor Hillary, nor Obama will be President, because very possibly, no one will be.

Yemen Post Newspaper

The funeral hall in Sanaa was destroyed.

Barack Obama: Ritual Murder in the Name of War

"While many Americans, myself included, were all hypnotized by the bizarre spectacle of the Republican nominee for president, a US navy destroyer fired a barrage of cruise missiles at three radar sites controlled by the rebel Houthi movement in Yemen.... this particular military engagement has the potential to drag the US straight into a protracted and escalating conflict...." Author Moustafa Bayoumi reports this in a London *Guardian* op-ed on October 15.

The U.S. strike was widely reported as retaliation for missiles that were fired at an American destroyer which failed to even reach their targets and did no damage.

"But we would also find that immediately prior to those incidents, on Saturday 8 October, a 500lb laser-guided US-made bomb was dropped on a funeral procession by the US-sponsored Saudi-led coalition fighting the rebels who, the Saudis say, are backed by Iran. This bomb killed more than 140 people, mostly civilians, and wounded more than 525 people."

Since then, the Saudis have admitted that "the on the ground intelligence was inaccurate." The Saudis regularly kill people indiscriminately in market-places, in funeral processions, and in wedding parties—in fact, in

any social formation that is pre-judged to be suspicious. (The Saudis spend the third largest proportion of money on their military in the world—more than Russia. The Saudis spend about 8% of their GDP on military affairs compared to Russia's 3.5-4%.) Their war has been vicious, without merit, a series of war crimes from beginning to end. There are reports from Yemenis on the ground to *EIR*, that several persons working for the perspective of peace through development of the New Silk Road may have been killed in the latest attack.

In a blog entitled "Obama Could End The Slaughter In Yemen Within Hours," the Black Blue Dog Website states: "Using U.S. support, [the] Saudi-led coalition fighting Iran-backed rebels in Yemen has been responsible for the majority of the 10,000 deaths there since the conflict began 18 months ago, and a brutal attack on Saturday that has reportedly killed hundreds. It has left more than 28 million people on the brink of famine. And it has allowed militant Islamists—notably Al Qaeda in the Arabian Peninsula, which is focused on targeting the U.S.—to seize more influence and room to operate than they have had in years."

But, as the Russians know first hand, it's not just Yemen, or Libya, or Syria where Obama's mass-murder in the name of war abides. It has been true since Obama first took office, increasing year by year. Nicholas Davies reported in 2012 that "Obama has overseen the largest military budget since WWII; an eight-fold increase in drone strikes; special forces operations in at least 134 countries, twice as many as under Bush; and a massive increase in the special forces night raids...which increased from 20 in Afghanistan in May 2009 to 1,000 per month by April 2011, killing the wrong people most of the time, according to senior officers."

It hasn't gotten better. Benjamin Powers reported in an article in May of this year, "Obama's 'Kill List' Is Here To Stay," that "in March of 2016, drones and other warplanes bombed an al-Shabab training camp in Somalia and killed about 150 alleged militants who were gathered at a graduation ceremony. Yet U.S. officials privately acknowledged that they didn't know the identities of those they killed."

Powers also wrote that "the program has little-to-no transparency in its decision making apparatus, and has even been called an extra-judicial assassination program, given the lack of due process provided to the targets, who in the past have included U.S. citizens."

Barack Obama: Joseph de Maistre's Executioner Redux

The Obama White House's approach to law, war, and life, bears closer resemblance to the French Terror under Robespierre, or the Spanish Inquisition under

---

Joseph de Maistre On The Executioner

"Who is this inexplicable being, who, when there are so many agreeable, lucrative, honest and even honorable professions to choose among, in which a man can exercise his skill or his powers, has chosen that of torturing or killing his own kind? Is there not something in them that is peculiar, and alien to our nature? Myself, I have no doubt about this. He is made like us externally. He is born like all of us. But he is an extraordinary being, and it needs a special decree to bring him into existence as a member of the human family—a *fiat* of the creative power. He is created like a law unto himself.

"Consider what he is in the opinion of mankind, and try to conceive, if you can, how he can manage to ignore or defy this opinion. Hardly has he been assigned to his proper dwelling-place, hardly has he taken possession of it, when others remove their homes elsewhere whence they can no longer see him. In the midst of this desolation, in this sort of vacuum formed round him, he lives alone with his mate and his young, who acquaint him with the sound of the human voice: without them he would hear nothing but groans. . . . The gloomy signal is given; an abject servitor of justice knocks on his door to tell him that he is wanted; he goes; he arrives at a public square covered by a dense, trembling mob. A poisoner, a parricide, a man who has committed sacrilege is tossed to him: he seizes him, stretches him, ties him to a horizontal cross,

he raises his arm; there is a horrible silence; there is no sound but that of bones cracking under the bars, and the shrieks of the victim. He unties him. He puts him on the wheel; the shattered limbs are entangled in the spokes; the head hangs down; the hair stands up, and the mouth gaping open like a furnace from time to time emits only a few blood-stained words to beg for death. His heart is beating, but it is with joy: he congratulates himself, he says in his heart, 'Nobody quarters as well as I.' He steps down. He holds out his bloodstained hand, the justice throws him—from a distance—a few pieces of gold, which he catches through a double row of human beings standing back in horror. He sits down to table, and he eats. Then he goes to bed and sleeps. And on the next day, when he wakes, he thinks of something totally different from what he did the day before. Is he a man? Yes. God receives him in his shrines, and allows him to pray. He is not a criminal. Nevertheless no tongue dares declare that he is virtuous, that he is an honest man, that he is estimable. No moral praise seems appropriate to him, for everyone else is assumed to have relations with human beings; he has none. And yet all greatness, all power, all subordination rest on the executioner. He is the terror and the bond of human association. Remove this mysterious agent from the world, and in an instant order yields to chaos: thrones fall, society disappears. God, who has created sovereignty, has also made punishment; he has fixed the earth upon these two poles: 'for Jehovah is master of the twin poles and upon them he maketh turn the world.' . . . (*I Samuel* 2:8)."

[From *St. Petersburg Dialogues*, quoted in Isaiah Berlin, *Crooked Timber*, pp. 116-117.]

Torquemada, than to the American Revolutionary and later Constitutional governmental forms invented by Franklin, Washington, Hamilton and their associates. The Tuesday "kill-in" is the distillation of the very nature of colonial rule, but with the quasi-religious notion of a "higher cause"—the "war on terror."

It is the moral opposite, in every respect, of the March 4, 1933 Inaugural address of Franklin Roosevelt ("the only thing we have to fear is fear itself—nameless, unreasoning, unjustified terror.") and of the Second Inaugural Address of Abraham Lincoln ("With malice toward none, with charity for all."). There is no sign whatsoever, there is no reason

U.S. drone killed 17 innocent civilians in Ra'ada, Yemen in 2013.

to believe, the the Obama Administration does not continue every Tuesday to carry out killings, including mass killing worldwide, as well as killings of American citizens. There is also no reason to believe that the kill list is to be discontinued when he leaves office. The institutionalization of the kill list is now the most enduring, efficient, self-reinforcing feature of the present legacy of the Obama Administration. Can you, in all conscience, say—especially when you hear what you have heard as reactions from the governments of thermonuclear powers China and Russia —that you can morally or physically afford one more day of Barack Obama, or what he represents, remaining in the office of the Presidency because of the lack of lawful, nonviolent action to induce the Congress of the United States to remove him?

The fact of that lawless killing being done under the pretext of "defense of the homeland," despite its being unacknowledged, has also had a great destructive effect on the psychology of U.S. domestic law enforcement, many of whom are former military personnel. Take for example the problem of the shootings and violence, as well as police violence, in American cities. To what degree has the resonance of eight years of drone killings, mass executions, murderous deposi-

tions of heads of state as in Libya, special forces operations, extraordinary renditions, and collusion with terrorist organizations we claim to oppose, seeped into the very fabric of American society itself? How much of the military suicide, mass shootings, and violence, permanently seared into the mind of the combat veteran or the veteran's family, including the children, is reflected in what we are seeing play out, in infinite variation, in the playgrounds and elementary schools, and on the street corners of America today?

If you issue kill orders each Tuesday under the pretext of fighting a war that you know is not a war, since you are regularly executing people that are not only not fighting you, but don't even know that they are about to die; a "war" where you yourself fund, equip, logistically support and even place and maintain in power your own enemy, including the people who have mass-killed Americans on American soil; a "war" where the intellectual and cultural heritage of centuries and millennia is permanently destroyed by laser-guided bombs that you have sold to people who have sworn to eradicate the very memory of the ancient civilizations of Africa and Asia, and whose victims on the ground you regularly, indiscriminately kill in funeral processions; if this be your behavior, can it be said that any human life matters to you at all? Can the real lives of the citizens of your nation, U.S. citizens that you have already been proven to have killed without due process with drones overseas, drones that you believe you have the authorization to use in a universal , imperial war on "terror" which includes the United States—can the lives of those citizens actually mean anything to you at all?

President George Washington's military was of a contrasting morality. He established the reputation of the American military as morally superior to that of the British on precisely the difference in the two armies' treatment of prisoners, and his general conduct of the war. Alexander Hamilton, Washington's aide, in his advocacy and participation in the establishment of the formation and deployment of African-American troop units during the Revolutionary War, and his fight for the abolition of slavery on the basis of the conduct of those men as combatants in that war, understood, unlike Barack Obama, what just war is, and what the conduct of lawful war entails.

But who does the executioner Barack Obama do his terror work for, if not for the "defense and safety" of the American people?

Barack Obama: British Functionary

Since its founding in 1782, British intelligence has worked to undermine the American Presidential system, even before it was created. Today's London, the center of world terrorism, financial crime, scientific fraud and Babylonian god-building (today called "celebrity"), continues in the footsteps of the East India Company of 1763 to target the United States as its mortal enemy. The revolution in 1776 America was intended to end all that. The Americans invented a new nation and a new economic policy—Hamilton's policy—which is still yet to be implemented today. Those first Americans recognized that the "Mother Country," exemplified by British Royalty, was actually "the Whore of Babylon."

Post-Revolutionary America, however, has had few great Presidents. Washington, John Quincy Adams, Lincoln, and FDR were the standouts. Hamilton was also a President "without portfolio." Others, such as the patriot Ulysses Grant, William McKinley, or John Kennedy, were fully justified in their proud opposition to Britain, although they were defeated in the execution of their intentions. When FDR died, the United States

Prescott Bush

Presidential system, through co-option, assassination, blackmail and misleadership, was and has been captured by these British interests more or less continuously since November 22, 1963.

The Bush family was the worst—that is, until their protege, Obama, became President. Without the events of September 11 and the subsequent eight years of Cheney-Bush, Barack Obama would never have been possible. It is the kind of inside joke of which British intelligence insiders are particularly fond.

The Bush family—especially the Nazis' American banker, Prescott Bush, with his personal relationship to the Dulles Brothers and Averell Harriman, husband of Pamela Churchill—is the center of British intelligence's managerial control of the American Presidency, especially from the time of the near-assassination of Ronald Reagan in March of 1981. Economist Lyndon LaRouche, author of the Reagan Administration's 1983 beam-weapons policy, ran a 1980 campaign for the Democratic nomination of President, during which he spoke at some length to the future President. LaRouche's campaign was central to the defeat of Bush's drive for the Republican Presidential nomination in the February 1980, New Hampshire primary. Bush was not happy with the outcome.

LaRouche was nearly assassinated on October 6, 1986, though actions of the same secret government apparatus that—through the 1980s Bush "41" Vice-Presidency, the 1988-92 Bush Presidency and Cheney Defense Department, and the Cheney/Bush "43" Presidency of 2000-2008—seized control of the Executive Branch from the American people. When that assassination setup failed, a series of pseudo-legal actions was initiated, and LaRouche was indicted in Boston in June of 1987. The case ended in a mistrial after several undisclosed documents showed the involvement of Bush "41" in direct operations against LaRouche. A second railroad was then begun against LaRouche in Alexandria, Virginia.

The American people were thwarted of the opportunity to elect LaRouche President after his 1987-88 judicial "railroading" by the Bush League. Former U.S. Attorney General Ramsey Clark, in a letter to then Attorney General Janet Reno on April 4, 1995, said of the LaRouche trial: "I bring this matter to you directly, because I believe it involves a broader range of deliberate and systematic misconduct and abuse of power over a longer period of time in an effort to destroy a political movement and leader, than any other federal prosecution in my time or to my knowledge."

LaRouche was tried in Boston, Mass., retried in Alexandria Virginia, convicted, and incarcerated from January 27, 1989 until January 27, 1994. That legal travesty was never corrected, and LaRouche became "factually impossible" to elect as President throughout the 1990s and afterwards. In 2000, the American people were adapted to the toleration of "virtual reality Presidents" by the Cheney-Bush "September 11 Reichstag Fire" two-term Presidency. Obama's two terms were the perfecting of the Satanic nature of that British "Sir George Bush" Presidential intention.

That can all now come to an end, if Americans simply choose to read, study and understand the works of Alexander Hamilton, and the LaRouche Four Laws' restatement of the Hamiltonian principle of economy, in time to avert the financial and military catastrophe that Obama "slouches toward Moscow" to give birth to.

Hamilton's works are imbued what poet Heinrich Heine called "der Liebe Geist"—the Spirit of Love that was the soul of Hamilton's fight against slavery, poverty, and injustice—against, in other words, everything "British imperialist." It was that same "der Liebe Geist" that Abraham Lincoln spoke about as "with Charity for all."

Hier sind nun die Lieder, die einst so wild,
Wie ein Lavastrom, der dem Ätna entquillt,
Hervorgestürtzt aus dem tiefsten Gemüt,
Und rings viel blitzende Funken versprüht!

Nun liegen sie stumm und totengleich,
Nun starren sie kalt und nebelbleich,
Doch aufs neu die alte Glut sie belebt,
Wenn der Liebe Geist einst über sie schwebt.

Und es wird mir im Herzen viel Ahnung laut:
Der Liebe Geist einst über sie taut;
Einst kommt dies Buch in deine Hand,
Du süsses Lieb im fernen Land.
—Heine, "Mit Myrten und Rosen"

(Here now are the songs which, once so wild,
Like a stream of lava that flows from Etna,
Burst from the depths of my heart,
And spray glittering sparks everywhere!

Now they lie mute and death-like,
Now they stare coldly, pale as mist,
But the old glow will revive them afresh,
When the spirit of love someday floats above them.

And in my heart the thought grows loud:
The spirit of love will someday thaw them;
Someday this book will arrive in your hands,
You, my sweet love in a distant land.)

The world awaits the United States that would return to that distant land from which Alexander Hamilton and Lyndon LaRouche's words have emanated—the real America. No more "Howdy Doody," "Bart Simpson" or "Freddie Kruger" Presidents. Simply remove them; you have not only the right, but the duty to do so, according to your Declaration of Independence. The ingenious, scientifically progressive, hard-working, generous, innovative, optimistic intention that was America, is only as distant from this moment as is the hand of the citizen, not from the voting lever, but from the pages of Hamilton's Four Reports. *Tolle Lege!*—"Take Up, And Read!"

Every Day Counts In Today's Showdown To Save Civilization

That's why you need EIR's **Daily Alert Service**, a strategic overview compiled with the input of Lyndon LaRouche, and delivered to your email 5 days a week.

For example: On Jan. 7, EIR's Daily Alert featured the British hand behind the pattern of global provocations toward war. Of special note is British Intelligence's role in instigating the Saudi Kingdom's attempt to set off a Sunni-Shia war. This religious war has been the intent of British strategy since the Blair-Bush attack on Iraq in 2003.

We also uniquely update you regularly on the progress toward the release of the suppressed 28 pages of the Congressional Inquiry on 9/11, which would expose the Saudi role.

Every edition highlights the reality of the impending financial crash/bail-in policies that would realize the British goal of mass depopulation.

This is intelligence you need to act on, if we are going to survive as a nation and a species. Can you really afford to be without it?

THURSDAY, JANUARY 7, 2016

Volume 2, Number 97

EIR Daily Alert Service

P.O. Box 17390, Washington, DC 20041-0390

- British Crown Pushing War and Genocide in 2016
- Financial Mudslide Goes On; Monetarist Tyranny Gloats over Bail-Ins
- Moody's Downgrades Portugal's Novo Banco
- Puerto Rico's Default: It's Every Vulture for Himself
- Wide Glass-Steagall Debate Set Off Again by Sanders Speech
- MI6 Mouthpiece Evans-Pritchard Touts Persian Gulf Chaos
- North Korea Tests a Miniaturized Hydrogen Bomb
- Uighur Terrorists Found in Indonesia
- Foreign Investors Are Flocking In to China

EDITORIAL

British Crown Pushing War and Genocide in 2016

Elect Hamilton's Principles, Not These Hand Puppet Partisans!

by Kesha Rogers

To cherish and stimulate the activity of the human mind, by multiplying the objects of enterprise, is not among the least considerable of the expedients, by which the wealth of a nation may be promoted.

Alexander Hamilton,
Report on Manufactures, 1791

Oct. 18—If you, the American people, want to free yourself from this horror show and nightmare called a Presidential election, you must refuse to be slaves to "party politics," what George Washington once described as the bane of our nation's existence. The American people must free themselves from the degeneracy of this nightmare and fight for a real solution.

Our people have long forgotten the principles on which this Nation was founded. Such principles of natural law benefit not one nation, but all nations. What the Nation and the world needs, is to "elect principles," the principles of economy of Alexander Hamilton on which this nation was founded, and which Lyndon LaRouche advocates, develops, and applies in his Four New Laws to save the United States.

These are the very principles and policies that governed the nation under the leadership of such Presidents as Franklin Roosevelt and John Kennedy, and Abraham Lincoln before them. They all understood what our nation was *not*—we are not a slave to an imperial system, namely the British Empire and its lackeys on Wall Street. It is time to put Wall Street and it protectors out of business. Shut them down, now!

This we can do by continuing the course set into motion many months ago, which led to the defeat of Obama's veto of the Justice Against Sponsors of Terrorism Act (JASTA). It was a defeat of the British/Saudi terror nexus run by the dirty money of the City of London and Wall Street. It is time to finish the job and shut down Wall Street and Obama now. Our nation

LPAC

must no longer be run by the corruption that killed Alexander Hamilton. We must set a new standard for value, as Hamilton did. We can start by defining and shaping the New Presidency, which LaRouche has set out to do in his four new laws.

LaRouche's solution, like Hamilton's, identifies that it is not money that constitutes value in an economy and in society, it is the increase in the productive powers of society through the advancement of the uniquely creative human mind.

The Principle of the General Welfare

The relevant principle—at the center of the establishment of our nation's Constitution, which Alexander Hamilton was instrumental in crafting—is the promotion of the "general welfare."

The very preamble to our Constitution declares,

NASA

At Cape Canaveral, Dr. Wernher von Braun explains the Saturn Launch System to President Kennedy, Nov. 16, 1963.

We the People of the United States, in Order to form a more perfect Union, establish Justice, insure domestic Tranquility, provide for the common defence, promote the general Welfare, and secure the Blessings of Liberty to ourselves and our Posterity, do ordain and establish this Constitution for the United States of America.

In Hamilton's *Report on Manufactures,* he refers to the general welfare as it is cited in Article 1, Section 8 of the Constitution, which states, "The Congress shall have Power To lay and collect Taxes, Duties, Imposts and Excises, to pay the Debts and provide for the common Defense and general Welfare of the United States." Hamilton then explains why the national legislature must have discretion to appropriate money for purposes of the general welfare:

The phrase is as comprehensive as any that could have been used; because it was not fit that the constitutional authority of the Union, to appropriate its revenues should have been restricted within narrower limits than the "General Welfare," and because this necessarily embraces a vast variety of particulars, which are susceptible neither of specification nor of definition.

He goes on to declare that "there seems to be no room for a doubt, that whatever concerns the general interests of learning, of agriculture, of manufactures, and of commerce, are within the sphere of the national councils, as far as regards an application of money." Hamilton specifies that such appropriations should be for the benefit of the Nation and not local efforts.

The principle of the general welfare, as defined in our Constitution's preamble, and the principle of the "pursuit of happiness," stated in our Declaration of Independence, are the very principles that are directly under attack right now by the murderous actions of an increasingly insane President Obama.

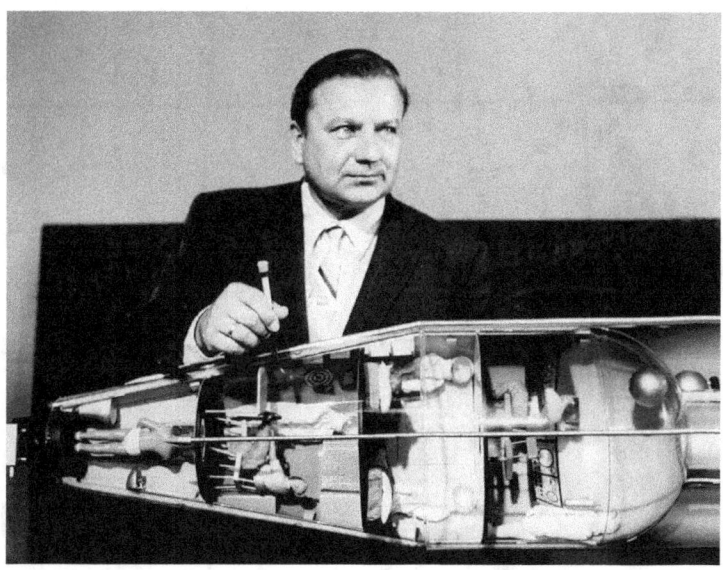

NASA

Krafft Ehricke demonstrates the plan for the interior of a space station.

Space Program: Hamiltonian Science Driver

This attack is explicit in his continued cuts in the funding of our Space Program and the mockery he has made of our nation's Space Program by attempting to turn it over to the commercial space industry. Obama is now advocating that the United States should rely on the private sector to get us to Mars. President Obama—at the White House Frontiers Conference held in Pittsburgh—shared the podium with Atul Gawande, a leading advocate for eliminating "excessive" healthcare in America, that is, he advocates killing people. At a conference where the nominal theme was innovative technologies, Gawande was there promoting a documentary, *Being Mortal,* associated with his book of the same name, on early death. In a recent article, he denounces the "epidemic of too much medical care" in the United States. He is no friend of advances in medical science.

That is what's at the core of the attack on the general welfare of our Nation, the idea of population reduction—killing off of the population, on the grounds that human beings are nothing more than talking animals. This was the fight around which our republic was formed in the first place: It was a fight between an obsession with the pursuit of property, and the ideal of the pursuit of happiness—the former promoting the slavery of a people, and the latter giving scope to the uniquely creative powers of the human mind to make discoveries, and therefore the promotion of the conditions of life necessary to make every human being free and creative.

President Kennedy and other great pioneers of space were directly inspired by Hamilton's principles for advancing the productive powers of labor through the advancement of human creativity. They saw that exploration and development in space are a necessary economic-scientific driver for the creative and productive powers of the human mind. This was certainly a field for promoting the general welfare of the Nation, a national endeavor for which federal moneys must be appropriated.

Taking Hamilton's Principles into Space

The great German-American space pioneer, Krafft Ehricke, understood the concepts of the increase in the productive powers of labor and the formation of a more perfect union. But he also understood that there are limits to how far these processes can go unless mankind

NASA

Astronaut Jack Schmitt on the Moon, during the Apollo 17 mission, Dec. 11, 1972.

leaves the confines of one small planet—Earth—and actually goes out to the far reaches of our Solar system and develops it.

What we come back to is the principle of the human mind, which is at the heart of Alexander Hamilton's writings, and of Lyndon LaRouche's elaboration of what a true science of physical economy is—which shaped his four new economic laws to save our nation. Krafft Ehricke describes the human mind as a force of reason. He writes:

State Administration for Science, Technology and Industry for National Defence, China

Krafft Ehricke: "I cannot imagine a more foreboding, apocalyptic vision of the future than a mankind endowed with cosmic powers but condemned to solitary confinement on one small planet." The far side of the Moon, as seen by China's Chang'e-5-T1 test mission launched in 2014.

We are cosmic creatures by substance, by the energy on which we operate, and by the restless mind that ceaselessly metabolizes information from the infinitesimal to the infinite; and, on the infrastructure of knowledge, pursues its moral and social aspirations for a larger and better world against many odds. Through intelligences like ourselves, the universe, and we in it, move into the focus of self-recognition. Metal ore is turned into information-processing computers, satellites, and deep-space probes; and atoms are fused as in stars. I cannot imagine a more foreboding, apocalyptic vision of the future than a mankind endowed with cosmic powers but condemned to solitary confinement on one small planet.

He goes on to apply the principle that Hamilton defined in his *Report on Manufactures* to the development of space, particularly to the development of what Ehricke calls our seventh continent, the Moon. He writes that taking manufacturing—and more broadly, the development of the process that organizes the increase of society and the formation of a more perfect union—beyond this planet, will actually start with the development and industrialization of the Moon:

Lunar industry should be viewed as an organism that, over time, evolves to progressively more complex capabilities and generates sufficiently strong foundations for expansion. Lunar industry must be broad-based and diverse if it is to last. The need for economic feasibility and early returns will require a skillful interplay between market/customer-oriented products and services, and infrastructural investments such as transportation, energy, and surface/space installations that expand food production and diversify industrial productivity.[1]

Hamilton's conception was not specific to one nation or one period of history. It is not even confined to one planet. His ideals are governed by natural law, for the benefit of all people and all nations. His conception was so organized—as Ehricke understood—that it applies whether we are on one globe, or we are polyglobal. If we are going to truly form a more perfect union, we have to free ourselves from a system of money and corrupt politics that keeps nations from developing. We must enact the Hamilton-LaRouche solution to rebuild and further develop our nation, and develop the entirety of the Solar system and the Universe. And only a productive society and the human mind can do that.

---

1. Krafft Ehricke, "Lunar Industrialization and Settlement—Birth of Polyglobal Civilization," in *Lunar Bases and Space Activities of the 21st Century* (Houston: Lunar and Planetary Institute, 1985), p. 836.

III. Financial Blowout Looms

Morale, Morality: Hamilton, Mozart— We Catalyze Our Fellow Americans

The dialogue between Jeffrey Steinberg and the Manhattan Project, Saturday, Oct. 15, 2016. These are edited excerpts.

Jeffrey Steinberg: It's a pleasure to be here, even if only by Google Hangouts. I just want to say at the beginning that it's imperative that coming out of this discussion today, everyone has a very clear strategic focus on our priority tasks. There's an enormous amount of distraction and literally a willful campaign to demoralize the American people by turning this year's Presidential elections into a pornographic TV reality show. There's a reason why major forces within the Establishment are trying to do that. We're at a point of grave crisis; the entire trans-Atlantic financial system is hanging by a thread. You could literally pick up the paper Monday morning, and find out that we're going through a Lehman Brothers shock, but a hundred times worse. Deutsche Bank is a major international bank; it's actually a City of London bank, it no longer has anything to do with Germany or with the prior tradition of Alfred Herrhausen and classical Rhineland German banking, industrial banking.

We also face the reality that President Obama, on behalf of the British and their Saudi allies, is attempting to provoke Russia, provoke President Putin through, again, a gutter propaganda campaign of lies with the intent of goading the Russians into taking a strategic step that would prove to be a blunder. That is not about to happen; Putin is far too smart

for that. The Obama forces, the British, the Saudis, are still reeling from the strategic defeat that they suffered, which all of you played a very critical role in, in the passage of JASTA; and then the overriding of President Obama's veto by an overwhelming bipartisan majority in both Houses of Congress. I can assure you that this is not something that has been accepted and minimized on the part of the Obama circles, the British, and the Saudis. After the override of the veto, the Saudis began doubling the amount of money that they're spending in trying to buy off and corrupt the Congress; so they know that this is simply the beginning of the end of their entire global terror empire operation.

More than Glass-Steagall

So, what are our priorities? In the discussion with Lyn and Helga earlier today, there were two things that became crystal clear. Number one, that we have got to

"The Obama forces, the British, the Saudis, are still reeling from the strategic defeat, in which you all played a critical role, in the passage of JASTA and the override of Obama's veto by an overwhelming bipartisan majority."

continue the drive for Obama's removal from office. If you simply consider the fact that he continues to conduct these Tuesday kill sessions in which extra-judicial assassinations are mapped out and signed on to by the President—including extra-judicial assassinations of American citizens; it should be very clear why it is that the very principles of our Constitution are jeopardized if this kind of behavior is in any way, shape, or form tolerated. Of course, by keeping up the heat, by forcing people to remember what the actual legacy of this President is, we go a long way towards making sure that he is denied any opportunity to blow things up even worse in his final three months in office. So, the removal of Obama, the demand that Constitutional principles be revived and this guy is removed, even in the very little time left in his Presidency, is something that carries a very powerful message.

Secondly, we've got to make sure that our strategic efforts are focussed on effectively establishing the same kind of emergency measures that were adopted by President Franklin Roosevelt in the first 100 days of his Presidency. And of course, as all of you know, the immediate reinstatement of Glass-Steagall is an essential element of that effort. But alone, Glass-Steagall doesn't do the job; it's a necessary first step, but we've got to insist on something much more than that. Namely, a full-scale Hamiltonian revival. Now, that's exactly what the legislative package that Franklin Roosevelt pushed through in his first 100 days in office accomplished; and we know the history of Roosevelt's own deep studies of Alexander Hamilton, going back to his own family legacy. One of his relatives was one of the closest partners and allies of Hamilton during the formative years of the republic after the Constitution. So, we've got that same task.

Keep the Laser-Like Focus

When Lyn wrote his Four Cardinal Laws more than two years ago, he was basically—as he has emphasized this week—putting forward a framework for applying Hamilton's core principles to the current circumstances that the United States faces. And of course, the situation globally, if you step back and look at the Earth as a whole, has shifted, so that a major center of gravity of real growth, of scientific and technological progress, is in Asia, extending into Eurasia. Western Europe, including Germany, is bankrupt; the United States is an economic basket case with a collapse of infrastructure. And now many of you have perhaps directly received word that Obamacare is in a state of disintegration. One of

"Who will be our allies in this fight to revive Hamiltonian principles, starting with Glass-Steagall?" Here, Alexander Hamilton.

our colleagues in Maryland received a letter which is typical of the letters received by over 1.5 million people just in the last several weeks, saying that the cost of their Obamacare health care is going to increase by 61% this year, and with a dramatic reduction in actual services provided. So, this is just typical of the general directionality of the collapse of our real economy.

So, it's this policy agenda that is vital to everything that we're doing. In all likelihood, there will be another President; and as we know very clearly, the next President is going to be problematic in the same way that the last two Presidents were very problematic, and worse. So, we've got to keep the perspective that the kind of laser-focussed mobilization that we accomplished that led to the victory in the JASTA fight, has to be carried forward. And the singular focus of that effort has to be on the implementation of a Hamiltonian recovery for the United States.

We Can Achieve a Major Breakthrough

Now, we're not starting from Ground Zero by any means. Both political parties have adopted Glass-Steagall in their platforms; and that was not just some minor thing. This was noted by Wall Street in a real reaction of panic, because of the implications of Glass-Steagall plus the other measures that Lyn has clearly laid out. So, that's the task before us. And one of the first challenges is to make sure that everybody's head is absolutely clear that the distractions that abound are not a diversion away from forcing people to face the reality that, unless we can succeed in implementing these kinds of major changes in policy direction, the country is doomed and future generations are going to be in very big trouble. And of course, the war danger is a byproduct of the desperation of those who are trying to hold together a system that's already dead.

www.fort-russ.com

Putin has outflanked all Middle East operations of the war party. The Syrian Arab Army, shown here, fighting further into Aleppo from multiple directions, is near to victory in retaking the strategically crucial city.

What we've got to clearly put on the table as a definition of leadership, which you're not getting from Clinton, you're not getting from Trump, you're not getting from anywhere else. We've got to define the policy agenda that must be adopted and implemented in the immediate period ahead. That is an underlying reality that basically has to be the driver for all of our work, because we can achieve a major breakthrough. The American people are hungry and desperate for the kinds of policies that we're putting forward. When we present these policies in a way that they understand what the historic roots are, that this is a restoration of the core principles upon which the American republic was founded, that we fought a revolution against a British Empire that is still the center of evil in the world today—we can make miracles happen.

So, Dennis, Diane, why don't we just throw things open now?

Putin Has Outflanked Them All

Dennis Speed: OK, let's go to the first question.

Question: This is J— from Brooklyn. I'm hearing what you're saying, and everyone in the room is getting,— you feel that tension from energizing ourselves to get ready for this fight. As a teacher, I noticed last week that in our mailboxes, there were *Time* magazines; the magazines are pushing this propaganda against Putin. We are supposed to be presenting these kinds of things in the classroom. Concerning Syria, it's saying that the Russians are preventing us from actually fighting ISIS. Yeah; how about that? And that Putin is trying to intervene in our elections. It's just crazy stuff! We *are* ready for this fight. I just want you to comment further on the strategy that we need, because the propaganda is outrageous; it's just everywhere. Where do we start and what needs to be done to intertwine impeaching Obama and getting Glass-Steagall?

Steinberg: I think there's a good reason why you have this effort at demonization of Putin; because with limited resources, Putin has successfully outflanked all of the war party operations around the Middle East. We're at a point right now in Syria where the Syrian government forces—with strong support from Russia— have completely cut off and isolated what's called the Aleppo pocket. This is the area of eastern Aleppo that's been in the hands of al-Qaeda; which is really the mother organization of the Nusra Front, no matter how many times they change their name.

Al-Qaeda has a last, remaining stronghold in that city; it's encircled, it's under siege, it's collapsing neighborhood by neighborhood. Everyone who thought that Putin was stupid, thought that the Russians would be drawn into Syria in a way that would make it another Afghanistan kind of trap. Putin has outflanked them all; it has now become clear that anyone looking for peace and stability in the Middle East—or frankly, anywhere throughout Eurasia—has to deal with Russia, has to work with Putin.

Ask Them, Do You Want Nuclear War?

You're going to see an even further round of hysteria coming out by the early part of next week, because what you're going to hear about is that the BRICS heads of state meeting has taken place over this weekend. Already today, there have been extremely important, bilateral heads of state meetings between Putin and Modi, between Putin and Xi Jinping, and between Modi and Xi Jinping.

That's just for starters. There have been massive agreements—both security agreements and vital economic agreements—expanding on the One Belt, One Road program, that are coming out of that whole discussion. There's actually, ironically, a piece in the *New York Times* today that begrudgingly admits that with a very small expenditure of resources, Putin has succeeded in having Russia re-emerge as a major global player. Last week, Putin was meeting with President Erdogan in Turkey, consolidating another major piece of their economic agreements, which are now part of an integrated Russia-China/One Belt One Road/Eurasian Economic Union process.

The propaganda you are referring to is all bluff and lies; and we've got to basically just dismiss it as exactly that. I think the question to pose to people when they raise all of this insanity about Putin, is to ask them, do they really want to start a nuclear Third World War? Because this kind of activity is leading in exactly that direction.

China Has Invited U.S. Participation

The fact of the matter is that Eurasia is organizing itself around Hamiltonian principles. At the very end of the 19th Century, the foreign policy of the United States was to build what today is called the Eurasian Land-Bridge. What Lyn and Helga called the Eurasian Land-Bridge, beginning at the moment that the whole Warsaw Pact and Soviet Union collapsed.

In the 19th Century, American military engineers were in Russia, building the Trans-Siberian Railroad with the Russians. Friends of the United States in the circles of Bismarck were building rail links from Berlin to Baghdad. In France, the American System faction around Sadi Carnot and Gabriel Hanotaux was building rail links from Paris to Vladivostok. So Eurasia had an American System concept back then that's now been revived by China, by Russia, by India. So the question is, why is it that the United States has abandoned its own concept of how to organize both our own economy and the economy of the rest of the world?

I think all of these things go hand-in-glove, and we're at a real inflection point moment right now, where people have to understand that it's really a choice between war and peace. In this case, peace means the kind of economic development that we're seeing emerging out of Asia in particular, but which can and must be integrated here in the United States. Remember when Xi Jinping initiated the development program and announced the launching of the Asian Infrastructure Investment Bank (AIIB), he made it clear; he made it clear to President Obama face to face, that China absolutely wants full engagement and participation by the United States in these efforts. That's simply an international corollary of what we've got to do in terms of a complete overhaul of our economic and financial policy at home.

A Brief History of *Time* Magazine

I know the second half of today's meeting is going to begin a detailed review of the major papers that Alexander Hamilton wrote as reports to the Congress. Those principles, as you read through them and look at Lyn's Four Cardinal Laws from that context, you'll see: Everything is there in conceptual outline for how to carry out a complete revival of the U.S. economy. And for the United States to join what used to be historically American foreign policy: Namely, encouraging the building up of infrastructure everywhere around the globe; the cooperation in scientific advancement; the things that are going on in Asia that used to be the cornerstones of why everybody around the world looked to the United States for leadership.

So, there's reference points for what we've got to do that I think are understandable to an overwhelming majority of our citizens. We've got to get people excited and engaged in thinking about ideas, rather than this process of dragging people down into the gutter, which is what the whole character of this Presidential campaign and the debates has been. And *Time* magazine—look, remember that *Time* magazine is the legacy of the Luce family. They put Adolf Hitler and Mussolini on the cover of *Time* magazine as world leaders to be emulated throughout the 1930s. So it's a scandal that *Time* magazine is being used once again to put propaganda together on behalf of war.

Our Years of Work in Congress

Question: Hello, Jeff. I'm Hans F—. I have a question which is actually two interconnected questions. There was obviously some strong relationship between

EIRNS/Sylvia Rosas

"Those concerts inspired many, many institutions—the firefighters, the police, the families, people who were fighting this fight for 15 years, and thought it was a lost cause."

the success of the passing of the JASTA bill and the choral process, the musical process going on here in New York—for me, specifically the four concerts that were done in connection with the 9/11 fifteenth anniversary. This relationship for me is not totally clear. It's clear that it's strong, but exactly how it works is not totally clear for me. That's my first question. My second question is, how would you apply that same process to get Glass-Steagall through and get Obama out?

Steinberg: On the first part of the question, there are details that some of us know about how the whole 28 pages and then JASTA fight played out. Some of it probably shouldn't be discussed publicly. From nine months before the 9/11 attacks—when Lyn gave testimony before the Senate Judiciary Committee on the confirmation of John Ashcroft as Attorney General—Lyn opposed Ashcroft, because of the emerging character of the Bush administration. He said, this is a government that will look for the first opportunity to stage a Reichstag Fire to go for dictatorship. So, nine months before 9/11, Lyn was forecasting on the basis of the

shape of that administration that was just coming into office, that this would the nature of what it would be like and what they would try to do. And of course, Lyn was being interviewed live when the 9/11 attacks took place, and again, it's another part of the history.

Our campaign for justice and getting at the full truth behind 9/11 had been going on for 15 years. The work that we did with Congress—I can just tell you—created the conditions for this to happen. People understood that Lyn was prescient in a way that no other living human being was about what was going to happen; what the Bush administration was like. And every single warning that we issued was absolutely born out—unfortunately—by the events that followed. So we developed an enormous amount of recognized credibility on that issue. Nobody could challenge us on the question of 9/11; why it happened, the elements that were involved in it.

They Saw the Way We Fight

Members of Congress, based on our work, literally, decided that this was a critical flank that had to be developed. We drove that flank through the mobilization around the 28 pages, around the JASTA fight. After Obama lied for seven and a half years that he would release the 28 pages, he was finally forced to release them, at the point that members of Congress said, we're ready to drop the "Gravel bomb" [former Senator Mike Gravel read the *Pentagon Papers* into the record from the floor of the Senate]: We're ready to just make it public on our own; and so, certain of Obama's aides said it's going to come out anyway, so why should you, who's obsessed and desperate for a legacy, be the demon in this story.

And of course, the buildup for the concert series, and the fact that it came off as effectively and as profoundly as it did, was a vital factor in the victory around the JASTA battle. Those concerts inspired many, many institutions—the firefighters, the police, the families, people who were fighting this fight for 15 years, and thought that it was a lost cause. They suddenly found that because of our commitment and the way that we carried out that fight, that something that they thought was impossible, was now suddenly possible.

And by introducing the intervention into the 15th anniversary of 9/11 through that series of concerts— that had a critical impact on everyone involved. You know, from being there, how much people were inspired. And since the question of willingness to fight is always a question of morale and morality, it should be clear that the miracle that we pulled off around those concerts, the quality of the performances, the impact that it had, was another factor that very much shaped the developments that ultimately led to that victory.

Americans Will Grasp the Four Laws

I think the larger lesson to be learned is that when Lyn launched the Manhattan Project back in October 2014, what he understood was that there was a certain quality of the population of the New York City area that was unique and could be a kind of a moral anchor for mobilizing the population of the country as a whole, and for impacting members of Congress who are under constant pressure to go along to get along. And today the kinds of despicable things you have to do to go along have gotten worse than ever.

So the fact that Congress, through an overwhelming, bipartisan majority, stood up to Obama, the British, and the Saudis, is a clear indication of what can be accomplished. But it requires all of those elements that we bring into the equation that nobody else brings into it. And so there have been two issues which, for the last number of years, have been the absolute, priority flanks that Lyn has wanted us to concentrate everything on: One was the Saudi fight, the 28 pages/JASTA, but really, it was a flanking assault against the entire Anglo-Saudi empire which controls this Obama Presidency and controlled the Bush Presidency before it.

So that was a critical flank and, as I say, they're more hysterical now than they were going into the JASTA vote, because they saw that Saudi money,— and I said this to some of the family members, "Saudi money can't buy shit anymore in Washington, D.C.," if it's held up against the kind of mobilization that we conducted, with Manhattan being a centerpiece of that effort.

We were able to assemble a combination of forces that reached way beyond our own immediate means, around a critical strategic flank that was in the interest of everybody. And that's exactly what we've got to do on the issue of Glass-Steagall, and the Four Laws and a revival of Hamiltonianism. This is an even bigger interest for the American people at large, because far more people understand that their conditions of life have disintegrated over the last 15, 16 years, than understand the details of 9/11.

Our Power Lies in Catalyzing Larger Forces

So if anything, we've got a broader constituency to reach out to on this issue, and we've got to be very attentive to the issue of morale and morality, in the same way that that was a driving factor in how we cumulatively created the conditions for victory on the issue of the 28 pages and JASTA. Because it's a much bigger victory. It was a punch in the nose to the entire British-Saudi empire, and it ain't over. You know, the 20th of this month is the first scheduled court appearance where the Saudis should be reinstated into the lawsuit by the families. There is a massive amount of evidence yet to be made public.

There are things that are going to follow on that. But we've got to make sure that we achieve an identical victory, using the same principles and methods. Who are going to be our allies in this fight around a revival of the Hamiltonian principles, starting with Glass-Steagall? You know, there are many, many institutions, and I'll tell you right now, in Washington, we are known from the standpoint of the two issues that we've strategically focussed on.

Every member of Congress knows that we created the conditions, with a number of individual members who adopted a responsibility to behave in a way that goes way beyond what they previously or normally did. Remember, Walter Jones was the guy who was so angry at the French when they wouldn't support the Iraq War that he renamed "French fries" to "freedom fries." And now he says that the two worst mistakes that he made as a member of Congress were supporting the Iraq War and supporting the repeal of Glass-Steagall.

So we've got to be the moral compass from which we create the combination of forces—we have the ability, Lyn has always emphasized this—to be the catalytic factor that activates and moralizes forces that go well beyond our immediate, direct reach and resources.

'Force People to Think in that Elevated Way'

So it really requires a certain amount of thinking on all of your parts, on what are the opportunities, where are the flanks, how can we broaden it, how can more and more people be brought into the fight around these core Hamiltonian-LaRouchean principles starting with the Glass-Steagall issue, which is before both Houses of Congress: There are bills in the House, there are bills in the Senate. Everything that we've done on these policy issues has been uniquely bipartisan, because these are issues that are in the interest of the entire nation, and this is where partisanship breaks down. Go back and read Washington's Farewell Address, in which he not only warns about foreign entanglements, but says the greatest internal danger to the United States is the emergence of parties and factions.

So we've got to be above that and force people to think in that elevated way.

Restore Glass-Steagall and Jail Criminal Bankers Before the System Implodes!

Michael Billington interviewed Daisuke Kotegawa on Oct. 8.

Michael Billington: Greetings. I'm Mike Billington; I'm meeting with Mr. Daisuke Kotegawa, and I'll give you a bit of a background on his career. Mr. Kotegawa is now the research director at the Canon Institute in Japan. He was, in the 1990s, one of the officers at the Ministry of Finance in Japan, who dealt with the late 1990s banking crisis in Japan; which we will discuss a bit here. He then became the executive director from Japan to the IMF for three years, I believe; at which point, we met with him. He's been a close friend of *EIR* and the Schiller Institute; he's spoken at several of our conferences, including the recent Schiller Institute conference in Berlin. He has been a strong advocate of the Glass-Steagall restoration; not only in America but internationally. We will discuss precisely some of those issues.

Let me ask first for you just to give your overview of the current crisis, eight years after the Lehman shock; and why you think we did not restore a sane banking system after that shock, and why we're now facing the crisis that we're in.

Daisuke Kotegawa: Well, basically, people in charge in 2008 in the case of the Lehman shock,— they were successful in stopping this crisis from becoming something like the Great Depression in 1929. But they made some substantial mistakes which we didn't do back in Japan in the late 1990s. The most important thing is, the authorities didn't arrest anybody among the bankers who were responsible for this big problem. From our experience in Japan, we know that bankers will just repeat wrongdoing again and again, which

EIRNS/Julien Lemaître
Daisuke Kotegawa

would give them big profits. So, the only way we can stop them, is to get rid of those people.

Billington: Which has not happened at all in the United States. Many people were arrested in Japan, and none here. Do you want to say something about the failure to restore Glass-Steagall and the failure of the Dodd-Frank bill to deal with this problem?

Kotegawa: Yes, the largest problem we have now is due to the abolishment of Glass-Steagall; now investment bankers can get involved in a huge amount of a kind of gamble, using ordinary people's money and deposits. These deposits are very, very important for the ordinary people; so the government cannot disdain these ordinary people's deposits. That's why the government has to maintain this kind of thing, a basic financial system. So, there's no other option for those governments but to bail those banks out in order to maintain ordinary people's deposits. Basically what happened in the past is, investment bankers actually privatized their own profits, while they nationalized the losses, and socialized their risk.

Billington: A very interesting formulation. Mr. Kotegawa is here in Washington because the IMF is having its annual summit here in Washington this weekend. Do you think that the IMF is going to be discussing any competent solutions; or do you think they're spinning their wheels trying to find some way of bailing out the current disaster?

Kotegawa: I hope they are, but I'm afraid they would not; because basically the IMF is a Europe-centered institution. They don't want to get these kind of problems exposed to the entire world. My deep concern is that the IMF cannot do anything.

Billington: The center of the current threat of an explosion is the crisis of Deutsche Bank, although many other banks are in similar if not quite as severe a situation. You have recently put forward a four-point proposal for what must be done if we are to prevent the Deutsche Bank uncontrolled collapse from causing contagion throughout the entire Western banking system, perhaps even in this month of October, I believe you said. Do you want to discuss that proposal?

The Way Out of the Crisis

Kotegawa: Yes, we have a way out; but before doing that, we need I think, two other conditions. That is, number one is the reintroduction of Glass-Steagall so that these kinds of mistakes will not be repeated; that's number one. Number two is the people who are responsible for these kinds of crises should be punished. Those are the conditions. We have to control this kind of bigger crisis; and this would require a very extensive cooperation of banking supervisory authorities

REVIVE GLASS-STEAGALL NOW!

"The point is, we need Glass-Steagall immediately. We need it because that's our only insurance to save the nation.... Get Glass-Steagall in, and we can work our way to solve the other things that need to be cleaned up. If we don't get Glass-Steagall in first, we're in a mess!"
—*Lyndon LaRouche, Feb. 11, 2013*

LaRouchePAC is now leading a nationwide effort to push through legislation for Glass-Steagall (www.larouchepac.com).

WATCH the LaRouchePAC video:
'Glass-Steagall: Signing a Revolution'

SUBSCRIBE to EIR Online
www.larouchepub.com/eiw
toll-free: **1-800-278-3135**
e-mail: fulfullment@larouchepub.com

of all countries where the counterparties of Deutsche Bank are headquartered. The first thing this group will have to do is to set, secretly, the specific day; where they are to settle all of these derivatives. Then, that would come down to the specific amount for each bank to get a bailout. So, all governments have to be ready to supply the required amount of money to bail out those banks.

Billington: On the condition that they implement the preconditions you mentioned; the Glass-Steagall and the arrest of the criminals responsible.
Kotegawa: Yes.

Billington: You have indicated that there's no solution to Deutsche Bank outside of those conditions, but that it has to be nationalized, that the German government has to give confidence back to the bank by putting the state behind it. How would that function? And do you think it will happen?
Kotegawa: Well, the banking sector is different from the manufacturing sector. In the manufacturing sector, it takes time for any manufacturing company to become insolvent; it takes 5-10 years. But the banking sector is basically a virtual world where the confidence in the system and also in a specific bank is very important. It is very important to make an announcement by the German government that the German government will be standing right behind this bank. The best way would be for the government of Germany to announce that they will partially nationalize Deutsche Bank, and ensure that this bank will not collapse.

Billington: Do you have any expectation that the German government is going to do that?
Kotegawa: This would be a big critical issue, which I don't know whether they are prepared to do it, because this big problem was created by the London branch of Deutsche Bank, where most of the employees are either British or American. The Germans are not involved, so when I visited Germany last June, I found there was much disinterest in rescuing Deutsche Bank; rather, one of the people said, "Let that bank collapse."

Billington: The impact of that, however, on the German economy would be devastating.
Kotegawa: No, the German economy is very healthy compared to other countries in Europe; but if Deutsche Bank collapsed without any control, that

would have, I think, a tremendous contagion effect on other major banks in Europe. I just will refrain from specifying the names of those banks, but I should say that about 10 to 15 major banks in Europe would become insolvent and disappear.

Billington: Mr. LaRouche's proposal, which is very similar to yours, uses as a reference the former CEO of Deutsche Bank, Mr. [Alfred] Herrhausen. How do you see the difference between Deutsche Bank as it functioned under the Herrhausen administration and previous to that, and how it has since that time?

Kotegawa: Well, if I just put it in a very simple way, that's the difference between a commercial bank and an investment bank. The investment bank does not create anything for the ordinary consumers, while commercial banks do not create huge amounts of profits for their banks. But they play a very important role to enhance the industries in certain countries. So, in a sense, I think commercial banks are very important for national economies and for their depositors.

The Source of Economic Growth

Billington: You've made a very strong point of the necessity of arresting the bankers responsible for having destroyed these banks. You indicated to me at one point, that in Japan the arrest of the bankers had an impact in lessening the banking community's impact upon the Diet, upon the parliament. How do you see the power of the Wall Street and London banks over the governments of Europe and the United States today, where of course, nobody has been arrested since the 2008 crisis?

Kotegawa: In 1997, the big crisis started in Japan, starting with the downgrading of the seventh largest investment bank in Japan — named Sanyo. Then, just three weeks later, the fourth largest investment bank of Japan, named Yamaichi, was also downgraded; and I was in charge [of dealing with the crisis]. The next year, two big major banks — one named Long Term Credit Bank, the other named Nippon Credit Bank — both of them were partially nationalized. Then all of the board members of those four institutions were later arrested and put in jail. That did not stop there, and supervisors like the people who worked in the central bank of Japan, the Bank of Japan, and also my clique in the Ministry of Finance; some of them were arrested just because they had too many occasions to have dinner with those bankers, or those securities houses. They were put in jail.

Some of my friends committed suicide and died; but in those days I thought those things were very cruel actions over those people. But after I observed here in the States what happened after the Lehman shock, I came to the personal conviction that arrest of those bankers was necessary to get rid of their big power over our Parliament.

Billington: There has been not a single person arrested from the banking crisis of 2007-8 in the United States; and in fact, the Department of Justice has explicitly stated that they had made the decision not to arrest any bankers. That it made it better for them to collaborate with the banks, rather than to arrest them. The result, I think, is now upon us. What is your concern about whether we can make it through this often fragile month of October; not only in the United States, but in the entire Western banking system? Or, do you think that this has reached a point that it cannot go on any further without either a collapse or a Glass-Steagall solution?

Kotegawa: Well, I was in charge of the investigation of those failed financial institutions back in Japan; and I found that those people who worked in banks didn't have any loyalty to their own banks, nor did they have any loyalty to their nation. Their interest was just for their own personal interests. Unlike in some people's imaginations, they are not smart people. Once they have a very good opportunity to have made fortunes in investment banking, then they really would like to repeat it. So, unless our authorities stopped them, it is highly likely that they would just repeat it. The government has to bail them out again and again, as long as commercial banking is linked with investment banking. I am not a U.S. citizen, but I had a chance to watch a very famous movie about Bonnie and Clyde; and they robbed a certain amount of money by attacking banks, but the money lost from this big crisis cannot compare with the scale of the money which Bonnie and Clyde robbed. They were shot dead, while people who are responsible [for this crisis] are not even put in jail.

Billington: Let me ask last, I know that you have, over your years of experience here at the IMF and otherwise, established very close friends around the world; across Europe, the United States, Brazil, Russia, China. As you know, in a very real sense, the world is divided between two paradigms now. One that you've described

—the general breakdown crisis, unrestrained speculation; and on the other hand, among the BRICS nations and the New Silk Road process in China, the emergence of a paradigm based on development, based on building infrastructure — railroads, water projects, nuclear power. And you have had some contact with some of the people involved in that paradigm as well. What is your advice to America and to Europe in terms of our relationship with this Russia-China-India nexus of nations and this New Paradigm?

Kotegawa: After this kind of financial crisis, the most important thing is to create real demand all over the world. Not just the money game, which has been enhanced by so-called "quantitative easing". Those emerging countries, including the BRICS, they do have a gap between their current economic living standard and the desire for a living standard. So this is a source of a big potential for economic growth in the future.

Billington: The United States generally gave up on investing on infrastructure in the rest of the world, or actually even within the United States. The argument being that this is better left to the private sector. The result seems to be that while the BRICS-centered nations, the New Silk Road countries are investing in huge infrastructure projects across Asia, South America, Africa; the US and European industries are very little involved in that process. How can we get the tremendous opportunity to the Western industries to recognize that this would be to their benefit, as well as to the rest of the world?

Kotegawa: To be very frank, I see there is very little space left for improvement in infrastructure, both in Japan and also in Europe. But that is not the case here in the United States. I must say that the highway system, the railroad system here in the States is inferior to their counterparties in China. China has much, much better railroads; they have much, much better highways. This kind of infrastructure can contribute a lot to the national economy.

Public domain/Sui-setz

U.S. infrastructure needs rebuilding to promote economic growth. The high-speed train between Tokyo and Nagoya, of the kind shown here, makes the trip in 90 minutes and there is a train every seven minutes. That distance is the same as from Washington and New York, but the U.S. "express" train takes three hours and there are only 20 trains per day.

Let me give you a very simple example. Between Washington DC and New York, now it takes three hours by train, the super express. The distance between these two cities is equal to the distance between Tokyo and Nagoya. With the Shinkansen [Japan's high-speed rail network], it takes only one hour and a half between Tokyo and Nagoya; while here it takes three hours. In addition to that, between Tokyo and Nagoya, we have those high-speed trains every seven minutes; every seven minutes with eighteen cars, and each one can carry 100 people. So apparently, if the United States had this kind of high-speed train system, that would enhance economic growth here in the States... this is really sad.

Billington: This is really sad. I'll conclude this. This is a time when we need to bring some joy to America, rather than sadness; which requires that we follow the sage advice of Mr. Lyndon LaRouche and of Mr. Daisuke Kotegawa. We're at a turning point in history, and our ability to implement sane policies that look to a future will determine whether or not this nation and Europe decline into a cataclysmic collapse and potential war; or whether we can actually revive that American spirit that was once looked upon by Japan and others, as a model for how to go forward.